RECIPES WITH SARDINES

EAT MORE SARDINES WITH THESE SIMPLE, DELICIOUS, NON-FISHY RECIPES

K. SUZANNE

*Green
Butterfly
Press*

ABOUT THE AUTHOR

Kristen Suzanne is an author traveling the world with her family on a multi-year odyssey to experience other cultures and stay fit while she stuffs her face with their food. (For now, meat anyway.)

Kristen's blog at: GlobalKristen.com

Twitter: @KristensRaw

Instagram: global_kristen

CONTENTS

OTHER BOOKS BY K. SUZANNE

The Carnivore Diet Handbook

Sardine Solution

INTRODUCTION

For a free, printable .PDF of the recipes in this book, email me at kristen@globalkristen.com.

Canned sardines have become more popular, as people realize what a cool and convenient protein they are. Their nutrition is fantastic. They make cooking easier. They're great for travel. Sardines are a delicious, easy-to-use, protein in a can. I think of them as a mom's dream food. I can whip them into an easy meal and I can use them to stay fit and healthy.

While I love the convenience of sardines straight from the can, I also enjoy dressing them up with the delicious recipes in this book. If you have kids or a partner who doesn't value sardines as much as they should be, then serving them in these recipes will surely make them fans. Sardines make an excellent breakfast, lunch, dinner, or snack, so enjoy them any time you get the urge!

Sardines are very versatile. In addition to eating them straight from the can, you can broil, bake, grill, purée, stir-fry them, and more. You can toss them on salads for an immediate protein boost or make delicious pâtés to eat with vegetables or your favorite crusty sourdough bread. They're even fun to just add to pizza, sandwiches, and eggs, giving the meal a turbo-charged nutrition boost.

Canned sardines come in a variety of flavors and options. The canned fish section of your local grocery store will usually have canned sardines packed in many different oils and sauces. You can find canned sardines that are packed in water, olive oil, lemon with olive oil, tomato (marinara) sauce, spicy red sauce, spicy chili sauce, herbs, and more. The fish is usually smoked, but on occasion they're cooked some other way that imparts no smokey flavor. We prefer the smoked variety, but we eat them all. Lastly, you'll see some cans of sardines that include the skin and bones (both of which are fine to eat), and others that are skinless and boneless. They are all ready-to-eat and require no cooking, but naturally you can add them to dishes that you cook, as well.

In most of the following recipes, it's your choice as to which "flavor" of sardines to use because the recipes are versatile. I typically pick canned sardines with the bones and skin, because they have more diverse nutrients. However, they are a bit different in texture with the bones (unless you purée them, in which case, you can't tell the difference). They are usually a bit stronger in flavor too, so that's personal preference.

If you or someone in your family are "sardine shy," many of these recipes are great for dialing down the sardines' fish flavor. For those folks, you might want to start out with the skinless, boneless variety.

Either way, there are plenty of ways to add sardines into your diet. This book provides you with twenty delicious recipes to get you started!

ONE

AVOCADO, SEA SALT, AND SARDINES ON BREAD

Yield 1 to 2 servings

Avocado and sardines are a great combination. You get a satisfying meal with healthy protein and fat. Sometimes, I just eat this mash straight from the bowl.

- 2 cans sardines, your choice of flavor, drained
- Zest from one-quarter of 1 lime
- Squeeze fresh lime juice, more to taste
- 1 avocado, peeled, pitted, and chopped
- Freshly ground black pepper, to taste
- Sea salt, to taste
- 2 to 3 slices of your favorite bread, toasting optional

Place the sardines in a small to medium-sized bowl.

Add the zest, lime juice, and avocado to the bowl. Mash with a fork.

Taste and add salt and pepper, as needed.

Spread on your favorite bread or toast.

TWO
SMOKED SARDINE CREAMY PÂTÉ
(ON TOAST)

Yield 1 to 2 servings

- 2 cans sardines, your choice of flavor, drained
- 1/4 cup whole-fat Greek yogurt
- Squeeze fresh lemon juice
- 1 green onion, chopped
- 1/4 teaspoon garlic powder, more to taste
- Sea salt, to taste
- Freshly ground black pepper, to taste
- Your favorite bread, toasted

Place the sardines in a small to medium-sized bowl.

Add the yogurt, lemon juice, green onion, and garlic powder to the bowl. Mash with a fork.

Taste and add salt and pepper, as needed.

Spread on your favorite bread or toast.

THREE

BOURSIN CHEESY SARDINES ON APPLES OR CUCUMBERS

Yield 1 to 2 servings

Boursin cheese is one of the best things ever made. You can find it in most stores. It's an addictive cheese spread filled with herbs and garlic. I have used it on everything from pasta to toast to stew to steak. Here, I use it with sardines!

- 2 cans sardines, your choice of flavor, drained
- 1/4 cup Boursin cheese, more if desired!
- 1 cucumber or apple, sliced into thick discs

Place the sardines in a small to medium-sized bowl.

Add the Boursin cheese to the bowl. Mash with a fork.

Spread on apple or cucumber slices.

FOUR

SARDINE SALAD WITH CREAMY HERB BALSAMIC VINAIGRETTE

Yield 1 to 2 servings

Balsamic vinegar is one of my favorites, and using it for this salad, topped with canned sardines, is perfect. I like using romaine lettuce, with sardines and a creamy dressing like this, because it holds up well to their weight. It's also crisp and refreshing.

Dressing Ingredients

- 1/4 cup balsamic vinegar
- 1/2 cup olive oil
- 1/2 teaspoon sea salt, more to taste
- 1 small clove garlic, peeled
- 1 sprig fresh rosemary and fresh thyme, finely chopped
- 2 squirts yellow mustard
- 2 tablespoons whole-fat, plain yogurt (or heavy cream)
- Freshly ground black pepper, to taste

Dressing Instructions

Blend everything.

Salad Ingredients

- 1/2 head romaine lettuce, chopped
- 1 to 2 cans sardines, your choice of flavor, drained
- 1 green onion, chopped
- 1/2 red or orange bell pepper, seeded and chopped
- 1 handful chopped walnuts or pecans
- 1 small handful dried cranberries or raisins

Place the lettuce on a plate (or divided by two, if you're serving two people).

Add the remaining salad ingredients on top of the lettuce.

Drizzle the dressing on top of the salad. Store any remaining dressing in a sealed container in the refrigerator for up to 4 days.

FIVE

SARDINES & SCRAMBLED EGGS

Yield 1 serving

Here is your breakfast for champions, served alongside a cup of coffee, of course. Double or triple the recipe for more servings.

- 2 eggs
- 1 tablespoon butter (for scrambling the eggs)
- 1 can sardines, your choice of flavor, drained and chopped
- 2 pinches finely chopped fresh rosemary
- Hot sauce, to taste
- Sea salt, to taste
- Freshly ground black pepper, to taste

Scramble the eggs in the butter until desired doneness is achieved.

Transfer to a bowl or plate for serving.

Top with sardines and rosemary.

Splash a little hot sauce on top.

Season with salt and pepper.

SIX

ITALIAN SARDINE CRUMBLE WITH YOGURT

Yield 1 to 2 servings

This crumble is like fish cakes gone comfort food. Serve in a bowl with a big spoon.

- 2 cans sardines, your choice of flavor, drained
- 2 tablespoons crushed crackers or bread crumbs
- 3 tablespoons freshly grated Parmesan cheese
- 1 tablespoon freshly chopped Italian parsley
- Squeeze of fresh lemon juice
- ¼ teaspoon dried basil
- 1 tablespoon softened butter, plus more for cooking
- 1 egg
- Sea salt and freshly ground black pepper, to taste
- 1/2 cup whole-fat Greek yogurt

Place the sardines into a medium-sized mixing bowl.

Add the crushed crackers, cheese, parsley, lemon juice, basil, butter, egg, salt and pepper. Mash it together with a fork.

Get a skillet heated over medium-high heat. Add some butter for cooking.

Add the sardine puree and let it brown a bit before stirring. Then, stir it around and cook it until warmed through.

Serve with yogurt on top.

SEVEN

SARDINE & BACON STUFFED BAKED POTATO

Yield 1 serving

- 1 russet baked potato, baked and sliced open*
- 1 to 2 tablespoons salted butter
- 2 slices bacon, already cooked and chopped
- 1 can sardines, your choice of flavor, drained
- 1 to 2 tablespoons sour cream
- 1/4 green onion, chopped
- 1 teaspoon freshly chopped parsley
- Sea salt and freshly ground black pepper, to taste

Place your baked potato on a plate. Add the butter and let it melt from the heat of the potato. Add the bacon.

Top the potato with sardines, sour cream, green onion, and parsley. Add salt and black pepper, to taste.

* Directions for baking a potato:

Preheat the oven to 425 degrees F.

Wash the potato, scrubbing any dirt away. Pat the potato dry with a paper towel. Pierce the potato with a fork or knife a few times. Rub olive oil all over the potato.

Bake for about 45 minutes on a baking sheet. Test for doneness, by a knife sliding into the potato without resistance.

EIGHT

THE SIMPLE SARDINE PROTEIN SANDWICH

Yield 1 serving

- 2 slices of your favorite artisan bread
- 1 to 2 teaspoons Dijon mustard
- 1 tablespoon butter, softened
- 1 to 2 leaves lettuce, cut to fit sandwich
- 1 dill pickle, sliced into discs
- 1 can sardines, your choice of flavor, drained
- Freshly ground black pepper, to taste

Spread the mustard on one slice of the bread. Spread the butter on the other slice.

Add the lettuce to the slice with butter. Add the sliced pickle.

Add the sardines on top of the sliced pickle.

Add some freshly ground black pepper.

Add the other slice of bread. Cut the sandwich in half.

NINE

BROILED JALEPEÑO SARDINES

Yield 1 serving

- 1 can sardines, packed in olive oil
- 1/2 to 1 jalepeño, sliced
- 2 dashes chili powder
- Squeeze fresh lime juice
- Flaky sea salt

Place the sardines, and the oil from the can, in a small oven-safe dish (like a ramekin). Cut the sardines in half, if needed.

Add the sliced jalepeño on top, and sprinkle with chili powder.

Broil for 1 to 2 minutes.

Add fresh squeezed lime juice and a pinch of flaky sea salt. Serve.

TEN

SARDINE GRILLED CHEESE SANDWICH

Yield 1 serving

One of the easiest ways to get your family to eat sardines is in a grilled cheese.

- 1 can sardines, your choice of flavor, drained
- 2 slices of your favorite bread
- 2 tablespoons butter, softened
- 2 slices of your favorite cheese
- Ketchup or mustard, for dipping (optional)

Spread the butter on one side of each slice of bread.

Heat a medium-sized skillet over medium-high heat.

Put a slice of bread in the skillet, buttered side down. Place one slice of cheese on top of the bread.

Lay the sardines on top of the cheese. Add the other slice of cheese on top of the sardines.

Top with the other slice of buttered bread, putting it on top with the butter side up.

Let it cook for a few minutes and flip. Cook a few more minutes and flip again. Keep an eye on the heat so it doesn't burn and flip a few more times to get the cheese melted and the bread golden brown.

When it's done cooking, remove it from the skillet to a plate. Cut in half and serve with ketchup or mustard for dipping.

ELEVEN

PIZZA WITH SARDINES

Yield 2 to 4 servings

Sardines are a great way to amp up the nutrition on pizza. This recipe is easiest when you simply add your canned (drained) sardines to the top of a home-delivered or frozen pizza that you heat in the oven. I admit, that's usually how I roll. Or you can make your own pizza using pre-made dough. Below are directions for all three methods.

"Cook Yourself" Pizza Recipe

- 1 pre-made pizza dough, ready to roll out and cook
- Pizza or marinara sauce from a jar
- Shredded mozzarella cheese
- 1 to 2 cans sardines, your choice of flavor, drained and chopped

Preheat the oven per the instructions on the dough.

Roll out the pre-made dough into a circle or rectangle.

Spread a layer of marinara or pizza sauce on top.

Add shredded mozzarella cheese.

Add the sardines. (You can add these before or after cooking.)

Bake per the instructions for the dough.

Remove from the oven, slice and serve.

"FROZEN PIZZA" Recipe Instructions

Begin heating your frozen pizza per the instructions.

While the pizza is heating, cut 1 to 2 cans of drained sardines (the flavor of your choice) into bite-size chunks.

3 minutes prior to removing the pizza from the oven, top it with the sardine chunks.

Heat the pizza for three more minutes.

Slice and serve.

"DELIVERED PIZZA" Instructions:

1. Call for pizza delivery.
2. While waiting for the pizza to arrive, drain and segment the sardines from 1 or 2 cans into bite-size chunks. Warm the chunks in the toaster oven or regular oven.
3. Once pizza arrives, top with the heated sardines.
4. Serve.

TWELVE

SARDINES WITH ORANGE, FENNEL, AND CAPERS

Yield 1 to 2 servings

The wonderful brininess of capers, sweetness from the orange, and the crunch of fennel make this combo especially tasty.

- 2 cans sardines, packed in water or olive oil, drained and chopped
- 1/4 cup diced fennel bulb
- Zest from 1/4 of orange
- 1 orange, peeled, seeded, segmented and chopped
- 1 tablespoon capers
- 1/4 to 1/2 green onion, chopped
- 1 tablespoon olive oil
- Sea salt and freshly ground black pepper, to taste

Place all of the ingredients in a bowl and gently toss to mix.

Enjoy straight from the bowl or on top of a salad.

THIRTEEN
RADISH CREAM CHEESE SARDINES

Yield 1 to 2 servings

The delicious intense cream cheese and the bite from the radishes is perfect with sardines. Enjoy this with toast or vegetable crudité. Or, perhaps, you'll just eat it straight from the bowl with a spoon, like I do.

- 1/4 cup diced radishes
- 4 ounces cream cheese, softened
- squeeze fresh lemon juice
- 1/8 to 1/4 teaspoon sea salt, more to taste
- 1/4 teaspoon dried dill
- freshly ground black pepper, to taste
- 1 can sardines, packed in water or olive oil, drained

Combine everything but the sardines in a bowl, and mix well.

Gently mix in the sardines.

Chill for an hour or so before serving, if desired.

Serve with raw vegetable crudité or your favorite toasted bread.

FOURTEEN

KETCHUP, MUSTARD, AND RELISH SARDINES IN A HOT DOG BUN

Yield 2 servings

Sometimes you just want some old-fashioned ketchup, mustard, and relish with your sardines. Serve it all on a hot dog bun, and kids especially like it.

- 2 cans sardines, packed in water or olive oil, drained
- 2 tablespoons ketchup
- 2 tablespoons yellow mustard
- 4 tablespoons sweet pickle relish
- 2 tablespoons chopped Italian parsley
- sea salt and freshly ground black pepper, to taste
- 2 tablespoons butter, softened
- 2 toasted hot dog buns

Toast the hot dog buns and spread the butter on them.

Spread or squirt 1 tablespoon each of the ketchup and mustard on each hot dog bun.

Add the sardines to each hot dog bun.

Top with the relish and parsley.

Add a little sea salt and black pepper to taste, if desired

FIFTEEN

TAMARI GINGER SARDINES AND RICE

Yield 1 serving

This recipe has an Asian punch of flavors to mix things up a bit. When looking for extra spice, use sardines that are packed in spicy oil.

- 1 to 2 cans sardines, packed in olive oil or spicy oil
- 1 green onion, chopped
- 1/4 to 1/2 teaspoon freshly grated ginger
- 1 tablespoon tamari
- 1/2 cup hot, cooked rice

Get a small skillet warm over medium heat. Drain the oil from the sardines into the skillet, and set the sardines aside. Add the green onion and ginger, and let it cook for a few minutes.

Add the sardines to the skillet. Briefly stir to warm the sardines and mix everything together. It's okay if the sardines break into chunks.

Add the tamari. Continue cooking until the sardines are warmed all the way through.

Put some freshly cooked, hot rice into a bowl. Top it with the sardine mixture.

SIXTEEN
MELTED CHEESY SARDINES

Yield 1 to 2 servings

My husband says everything is better with melted cheese. Sardines, too? Sure!

- 2 cans sardines, packed in tomato sauce
- 1/8 teaspoon dried oregano
- 1/4 cup shredded mozzarella cheese
- 1 tablespoon freshly grated Parmesan cheese
- 1 tablespoon freshly chopped parsley

Put the sardines, and their accompanying tomato sauce, into an oven-safe dish. A ramekin is perfect.

Add the oregano and top with the two cheese.

Place the oven-safe dish under the broiler or in a toaster oven for a few minutes to warm the sardines and melt the cheese.

Top with parsley and serve.

SEVENTEEN

BUTTERY SARDINE SMASH WITH SUN-DRIED TOMATOES & OLIVES

Yield 1 to 2 servings

My husband might say everything is better with cheese, but I say the same for butter.

This recipe is great served as a filling for a sandwich or toss it into freshly cooked hot pasta!

- 2 cans sardines, your choice of flavor, drained and chopped
- 2 tablespoons butter, softened (or more!)
- 2 tablespoons chopped sun-dried tomatoes
- 4 Kalamata olives, pitted and chopped
- 2 tablespoons freshly chopped basil
- Sea salt and freshly ground black pepper, to taste

Using a fork, smash everything together in a bowl.

Serve with bread, toast, crackers, or over hot pasta. (If I serve this over pasta, I like to add extra butter.)

EIGHTEEN
SALSA SARDINES

Photo: See cover

Yield 1 to 2 servings

Salsa and sardines make a great combination. My favorite kinds of salsa always have a bit of spice and pineapple in them! This is great eaten straight out of the bowl or dipping corn chips into it.

- 2 cans sardines, packed in water or olive oil, drained
- 3 slices lemon for garnish
- 1 cup of your favorite jarred salsa
- 1 tablespoon freshly chopped cilantro or parsley
- Corn chips (blue, white, or yellow), optional

Drain the sardines and cut them into chunks.

Put the salsa in a shallow bowl, and add the sardines.

Top with cilantro or parsley. Enjoy with corn chips.

NINETEEN

FRANK'S SAUCE AND SARDINES

Yield 1 to 2 servings

This is a sauce I make that my family loves. We use it on burgers, vegetables, and sardines.

Years ago, I used to eat at *Frank's*, a little fish restaurant in Fenton, Michigan. They always had a delicious orange-colored sauce on the table. This is my best attempt to recreate it, having no idea what was in the original version.

- 2 cans sardines, packed in water or olive oil, drained
- 3 tablespoons whole-fat greek yogurt
- 2 tablespoons ketchup
- 2 teaspoons mustard
- 1 tablespoon capers
- 1 teaspoon minced chives

Place all of the ingredients in a small to medium-sized bowl.

Smash them up together. Enjoy on thickly sliced crusty bread.

TWENTY

SURF-N-TURF LETTUCE WRAPS

Yield 2 servings

The freshness of the lettuce wraps is perfect for the sardine and beef filling that goes inside.

- 2 cans sardines, your choice of flavor, drained and chopped
- 1/2 pound (8 ounces) ground beef
- 1/2 teaspoon chili powder
- 1/2 teaspoon onion powder
- 1/4 teaspoon garlic powder
- Squeeze fresh lime juice
- Sea salt and freshly ground black pepper, to taste
- 2 to 4 large romaine lettuce leaves

Season the ground beef with salt and pepper.

Add the ground beef to a small skillet with the chili powder, onion powder, and garlic powder.

Cook the ground beef, crumbling it with a spatula as it cooks.

Once the beef is cooked to your liking, add the sardines and cook until the sardines are warmed through.

Place the lettuce leaves on two plates. Divide the surf-n-turf mixture and place in the lettuce wraps.

Squeeze fresh lime juice on top.

FREE PDF

For a free, printable .PDF of the recipes in this book, email me at kristen@globalkristen.com.

Did you enjoy this book? If so, please leave a review!

As an independent author, your reviews are extremely helpful in getting the word out. After you leave a review, please drop me a line at kristen@globalkristen.com so I can thank you!

Other books by Kristen Suzanne:

The Carnivore Diet Handbook

Sardine Solution

Kristen's blog at: GlobalKristen.com

Twitter: @KristensRaw

Instagram: global_kristen

Made in the USA
Middletown, DE
06 June 2019